The

WHAT IF GAME

A Self-Progress Journal
For Abundant Success

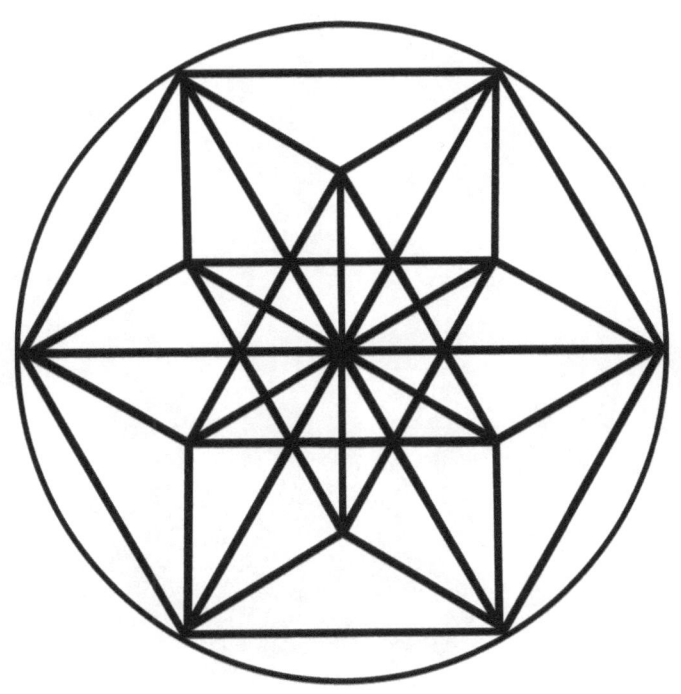

Courtney Lee

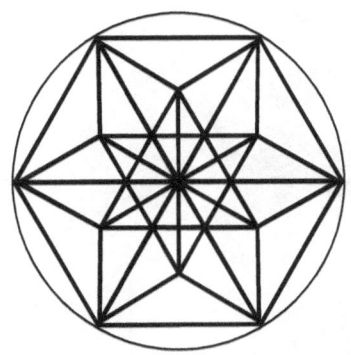

What if you could rewire your brain for success?

What if everything you've been searching for—clarity, confidence, and purpose—was already within you, just waiting to be activated?

In the following pages, you'll embark on a journey of self-discovery, using the science of manifestation to reshape the way you think, act, and create opportunities in your life. Step by step, you'll tap into your innate ability to achieve abundant success on your own terms.

Are you ready?

This journal belongs to:

_____

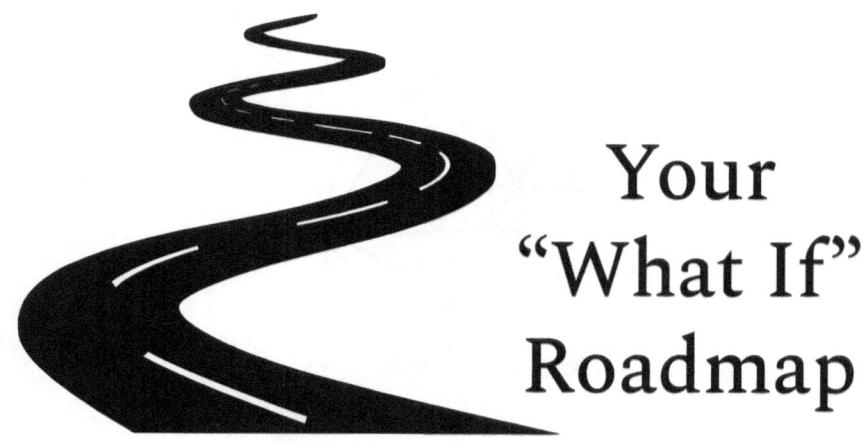

Your "What If" Roadmap

First, we'll start with facing the fears of our worst case scenarios and create logical escape hatches.

Then, we'll envision the dream and define abundant success.

Finally, we'll use all the senses to embody what the dream of abundant success becoming a reality will feel like.

Starting with intention

What if I turn my dream of abundant success into a reality?

My dream is:

_____

_____

_____

_____

_____

_____

_____

_____

_____

What is the shape and hue of your dream's energy?

Use the isometric grid to sketch below. This grid is featured throughout your journal as a space for meditative precision sketching. By engaging with this practice, you can align with the energy of your dream, translating its essence into form.

Facing Our Fears

How long have you spent playing the What If game?

What if I fail?

What if it doesn't work?

What if I can't make it happen?

What if I don't have what it takes?

What if I embarrass myself by trying?

What if I'm not as qualified as I thought?

What if...

"A man who fears suffering is already suffering from what he fears."

Michel de Montaigne

Let's pause here and analyze how this line of questioning feels in your body. Did your heart rate increase? Did your breathing get shallow? Are your palms sweaty? (Knees weak, arms are heavy?)

Now consider:

Why does this happen every time you think about starting?

_____

_____

_____

_____

_____

_____

_____

How can we redirect these feelings into positive affirmations of trying anyway?

_____

_____

_____

_____

_____

_____

_____

When we consider all that could go wrong from going after the abundant success we truly desire, we plant the seed of doubt. This seed grows into a full-fledged freeze state that prevents us from starting on the very dream we want. Instead of doing the work to obtain that which we desire, we feel compelled to seek routine. We put off starting until Monday, or next week, maybe the time will be right next year. This unconscious procrastination is our brain's way of predicting our circumstances and therefore maintaining the illusion of safety. "Why is safety an illusion?," you might ask.

Predictable outcomes equate to presumed safety. We can't control circumstances outside of ourselves, so the illusion of safety is composed of the nets we cast that are the same ones we've cast before. Routines allow the brain to predict the outcomes due to a functional cluster of neurons within the neocortex of your brain called the basal ganglia. These neurons are responsible for the initiation of motor movement, so they make executive decisions on which actions to allow and which to inhibit.[1] This region of the brain acts a gate-keeping mechanism for unpredictable actions. Even if those actions will improve our quality of life, the basal ganglia cannot predict the outcome if we have never participated in said action. Therefore, we stick to our Saturday night routines, and put our dreams off until Monday.

Of course we know that anything can happen at any time, but if we keep acting in the ways we've always acted, we'll be fine, right? I don't know about you, but as a millennial, times have been unprecedented since I was in the second grade. We can never predict whether we'll be fine and in most cases we just end up back where we started.

So what if we just try?

The risk of trying for the dream of abundant success is never as great as the reward of building new neural pathways to help achieve our goal. The human brain's inherent neuroplasticity encourages repetitive affirmations towards a goal to bridge new neural connections that find ways to make our dream a reality. Your brain is waiting to be optimized towards your goal. Try coming up with an affirmation that overcomes the basal ganglia's desire of routine.

"The brain is wired to be two and a half times more likely to avoid risk than to chase reward."

Dr. Tara Swart

Practice your affirmations below:

(Example: I am willing to fail until I succeed at finding what makes my soul happy.)

_____

_____

_____

_____

_____

_____

_____

_____

According to Oxford, failure is the lack of success. According to Edison, failure is finding 10,000 ways that won't work.

What is your definition of failure?

(Example: My definition of failure is the lack of trying)

How would you overcome this fear of failure?
(Example: I would realize I have nothing to lose even if I end up back where I started)

_____

_____

_____

_____

_____

_____

_____

_____

How would you overcome obstacles that stood in the way of you and your dream?
(Example: I would learn from every mistake)

_____

_____

_____

_____

_____

_____

_____

_____

Acceptance

Now, we have a clear picture of our definition of failure and how we can overcome it. Did you find the logical escape hatch to your fears? I recommend pausing here and going for a walk if you need a break. Rumination is the death of progress and studies have shown that a short walk in nature, even a city park, can reduce negative mood and inspire more awe.[2]

Once we are feeling inspired to keep going, we can take the first steps towards the acceptance of where we are and how far it is from where we want to be. The idea is to see how much wisdom you already possess that allows you to advance toward your goal. Using our core values to guide the exercises in this journal, we will see we're closer than we think to achieving our dream of abundant success.

"We cannot change anything unless we accept it."

Carl Jung

What are your current setbacks preventing you from reaching your goal?

(Example: I lack the financial resources to advertise)

_____

_____

_____

_____

_____

_____

_____

_____

How can we find the strengths in the setback?

(Example: I can attend free workshops and build a network of similar professionals)

_____

_____

_____

_____

_____

_____

_____

What is currently within your control in regards to achieving your goal?

(Example: I can write each day until I feel confident to share)

_____

_____

_____

_____

_____

_____

What can you release?

(Example: I don't have to tailor my art to others, I am doing this for me)

_____

_____

_____

_____

_____

_____

_____

Envisioning the Dream

Now, if you're ready, let's flip the mental switch.

What if we did the thing anyway!?

What if it works against all odds?

What if they love it?

What if I get an invitation?

What if I become the inspiration for future generations?

What if I succeed?

What if...

"What if we try? We might just succeed, and even if we don't, at least we won't wonder what could have been."

Again, let's pause here and analyze how this line of questioning feels in your body. Did you sit up straighter? Narrow your eyes and focus harder? Did you allow in the energy of hope? What does this feel like for you?

"We don't create abundance. Abundance is always present. We create limitations."

Arnold Patent

I remember my abundance by:

_____

_____

_____

_____

_____

_____

and I deny my limitations by:

_____

_____

_____

_____

_____

_____

There's a functional system in your brain called the reticular activating system (RAS) that lives within the anterior section of your brainstem and is essentially activated through envisioning an outcome. This is the same system in your brain that shows you seemingly more red convertibles on the highway after you went and purchased a red convertible. Does everyone have a red convertible now or did you tell your RAS to pay closer attention to them? The latter can be explained by the functions carried out by the group of neurons that contribute to the RAS. They are responsible for attention, arousal, modulation of muscle tone, and the ability to focus.[3] Therefore, once this system is activated, the creative solutions-based part of your brain is focusing on exactly what you programmed it to pay attention to. You tell your internal "Explore" page what you want to see more of.

In the previous sections, we invited your mind to overcome your fears and limitations. What does this do? This exploration brings your attention and focus to solutions that will alleviate the very circumstances your procrastination is seeking to avoid. Let's keep working with the reticular activating system with another exercise.

**I am inherently abundant,
I will not create limitations.**

According to Oxford, success is the accomplishment of an aim or purpose and Mr. Living on a Prayer himself, Jon Bon Jovi, classifies success as falling nine times and getting up 10.

What is your definition of success?
Define success using as many details as possible.

_____

_____

_____

_____

_____

_____

_____

_____

_____

_____

_____

_____

And now let's take the same application of logic from before and apply it to our second set of "What Ifs"

What if, even though I'm scared, it works against all odds and the limitations I placed on starting are less cumbersome than I anticipated?

(Example: I will be relieved my hard work and preparation paid off)

_____

_____

_____

_____

_____

_____

How will it feel to overcome my fears?

(Example: I will feel accomplished in taking small steps toward my bigger goal)

_____

_____

_____

_____

_____

_____

What if my audience loves my contribution and thanks me for sharing my work?

(Example: I will know I am serving my community)

_____

_____

_____

_____

_____

_____

_____

How will I feel when my audience thanks me for my contribution?

(Example: I will be elated to have played a small part in inspiring someone else to chase their dream)

_____

_____

_____

_____

_____

_____

What if I do have what it takes to earn a living off of my dream?

(Example: I will quit my 9-5 and have so much time for _____)

_____

_____

_____

_____

_____

_____

_____

How will I feel when I am supporting myself (and my family) by chasing my dream?

(Example: I will have peace in knowing that we all deserve the rewards I risked it all for)

_____

_____

_____

_____

_____

_____

What if I get an invitation and they dream of working with me as much as I dreamt of working with them?

(Example: I will show up grateful and enthusiastic to share how they inspired me)

_____

_____

_____

_____

_____

_____

_____

How will I feel knowing I earned my seat at the table I'd been dreaming of?

(Example: I will feel fulfilled by setting and obtaining a vision)

_____

_____

_____

_____

_____

_____

_____

What if I become the inspiration for future generations and was able to tell them what I wished I would've heard?

(Example: I will know that I never gave up, even when the odds were stacked against me)

_____

_____

_____

_____

_____

_____

_____

How will I feel when my family tells me they are proud of what I have accomplished? What will I say to encourage younger generations?

(Example: I will thank them for their contributions to my journey and will encourage the youth to persevere)

_____

_____

_____

_____

_____

_____

_____

What if I succeed?

(Example: I will be a bestselling author and healer through empowerment education)

_____

_____

_____

_____

_____

_____

_____

How will I feel when I reach the point of success that shows me it was all worth it?

(Example: I will be grateful for my determination and discipline for my vision)

_____

_____

_____

_____

_____

_____

_____

Great job!

We have successfully envisioned our future.

We have created solutions to perceived obstacles using the basal ganglia and stimulated our reticular activating system to pay closer attention to our desired outcomes. Our minds are now actively forming neural pathways that hardwire us to see the opportunities present that enable us to get started achieving our dream of abundant success.

How are you feeling about your progress?

_____

_____

_____

_____

_____

_____

_____

_____

Envisioning the Dream

In this state of self-induced inspiration, let's create a vision board. This activity uses any medium of choice (drawing, cut outs, freeform) to further visualize the dream of abundant success we have defined.

The isometric grid offers a space of clarity and precision in bringing your dream from your spirit into your environment. The vision board represents your goals as images of inspiration. Engage your meditative ability of focus to bring the vision into the pages with as much detail as possible.

Embodying the Dream

"To truly dream is not to just see with your eyes, but to feel with your skin, hear with your soul, smell the essence of the moment, and taste the very flavor of your desire."

In the next exercises, we'll bring every one of our senses on board to embody our vision. In doing so, our bodies will begin to feel the future we're working to create. The abundant success dream that we've been dreaming gets to live outside of our mind and in every cell and microenvironment in our body. This means instead of thinking one thought towards reaching your goal, you're using the power of 30 trillion cells and 38 trillion bacteria to help you reach the goal.[4] The optimization of whole body manifestation is achieved through balanced nutrition, movement, mindfulness, and community. For more guidance on whole body optimization, visit my website WellnessWithoutWalls.life.

In the first section, using logical escape hatches, we were able to switch ourselves into a parasympathetic rest state. This process allows our minds, and therefore our bodies, to think more clearly and bring to light the very dream we've kept hidden in the darkness of our fears. Using this newfound illumination, we can manifest the dream of abundant success we crave, with all that we already are.

What does abundant success look like to you?

(Example: Abundant success looks like a vibrant, community serving calendar with scheduled time for play)

_____

_____

_____

_____

_____

_____

_____

_____

_____

_____

_____

_____

_____

_____

_____

What does abundant success sound like to you?

(Example: Abundant success sounds like birds chirping on the window sill in the gentle breeze of a slow morning)

_____

_____

_____

_____

_____

_____

_____

_____

_____

_____

_____

_____

_____

What does abundant success smell like to you?

(Example: Abundant success smells like fresh-baked sourdough bread wafting through the hallways of my home)

_____

_____

_____

_____

_____

_____

_____

_____

_____

_____

_____

_____

_____

What does abundant success taste like to you?

(Example: Abundant success tastes like prebiotics and probiotics in whole foods that support my gut microbiome)

_____

_____

_____

_____

_____

_____

_____

_____

_____

_____

_____

_____

_____

What does abundant success physically feel like to you?

(Example: Abundant success feels like the subtle stillness of a butterfly landing on my shoulder, aka a regulated nervous system)

_____

_____

_____

_____

_____

_____

_____

_____

_____

_____

_____

_____

_____

Embodying the Dream

In this state of self-induced motivation, let's create an action board. This activity uses any medium of choice (drawing, cut outs, freeform) to further embody the dream of abundant success we have defined.

The isometric grid offers the opportunity to sketch the movement of the platonic solids (fire, air, water, earth, and ether) necessary to bring your dream into your reality. We should include value-based actions that can be employed daily until we are exactly where we want to be.

I want us to imagine ourselves in the present, with all of our wisdom and tools, guiding the version of us that first dared to dream the dream of abundant success we're achieving. In the space below, include an image of (or a letter to) your younger self to remind you to make it as easy as possible for them to obtain their dream.

You both deserve this dream.

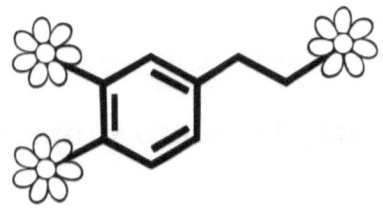

Inducing Dopamine
Week One

Now, let's continue to be self motivated with value-based progress tracking over time. This stimulates the well-deserved dopamine of keeping the promises you have made to yourself and your dream.

What are this week's value-based action steps needed to reach your dream?

Step One: _____

_____

Step Two: _____

_____

Step Three: _____

_____

Step Four: _____

_____

Step Five: _____

_____

How can we break Step One into simpler actionable steps?

_____

_____

_____

_____

_____

_____

_____

_____

_____

_____

_____

_____

_____

_____

_____

_____

_____

_____

How can we break Step Two into simpler actionable steps?

_____

_____

_____

_____

_____

_____

_____

_____

_____

_____

_____

_____

_____

_____

_____

_____

_____

_____

How can we break Step Three into simpler actionable steps?

_____

_____

_____

_____

_____

_____

_____

_____

_____

_____

_____

_____

_____

_____

_____

_____

_____

_____

_____

How can we break Step Four into simpler actionable steps?

_____

_____

_____

_____

_____

_____

_____

_____

_____

_____

_____

_____

_____

_____

_____

_____

_____

_____

_____

How can we break Step Five into simpler actionable steps?

_____

_____

_____

_____

_____

_____

_____

_____

_____

_____

_____

_____

_____

_____

_____

_____

_____

_____

How can we ensure discipline in these actions?

_____

_____

_____

_____

_____

_____

_____

_____

_____

_____

_____

_____

_____

_____

_____

_____

_____

_____

_____

_____

_____

What are your current wins towards reaching your goal?

_____

_____

_____

_____

_____

_____

_____

How can we ensure more of them?

_____

_____

_____

_____

_____

_____

_____

_____

_____

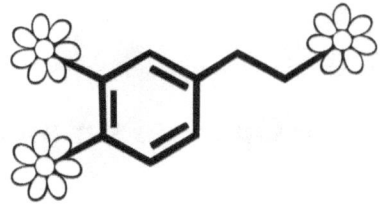

Inducing Dopamine
Week Two

As we begin the second week of dopamine stimulation, the actions behind the discipline should be increasingly easier.

What are this week's value-based action steps needed to reach your dream?

Step One: _____

_____

Step Two: _____

_____

Step Three: _____

_____

Step Four: _____

_____

Step Five: _____

_____

How can we break Step One into simpler actionable steps?

_____

_____

_____

_____

_____

_____

_____

_____

_____

_____

_____

_____

_____

_____

_____

_____

How can we break Step Two into simpler actionable steps?

_____

_____

_____

_____

_____

_____

_____

_____

_____

_____

_____

_____

_____

_____

_____

_____

_____

_____

_____

How can we break Step Three into simpler actionable steps?

_____

_____

_____

_____

_____

_____

_____

_____

_____

_____

_____

_____

_____

_____

_____

_____

_____

_____

How can we break Step Four into simpler actionable steps?

_____

_____

_____

_____

_____

_____

_____

_____

_____

_____

_____

_____

_____

_____

_____

_____

_____

_____

_____

_____

How can we break Step Five into simpler actionable steps?

_____

_____

_____

_____

_____

_____

_____

_____

_____

_____

_____

_____

_____

_____

_____

_____

_____

How can we ensure discipline in these actions?

_____

_____

_____

_____

_____

_____

_____

_____

_____

_____

_____

_____

_____

_____

_____

_____

_____

_____

_____

_____

_____

_____

What are your current wins towards reaching your goal?

_____

_____

_____

_____

_____

_____

_____

How can we ensure more of them?

_____

_____

_____

_____

_____

_____

_____

_____

_____

_____

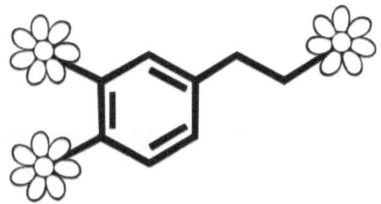

Inducing Dopamine
Week Three

The end of this week will signify the effective institution of a new habit (21 days) of working towards your dream.

What are this week's value-based action steps needed to reach your dream?

Step One: _____

_____

Step Two: _____

_____

Step Three: _____

_____

Step Four: _____

_____

Step Five: _____

_____

How can we break Step One into simpler actionable steps?

_____

_____

_____

_____

_____

_____

_____

_____

_____

_____

_____

_____

_____

_____

_____

_____

_____

_____

How can we break Step Two into simpler actionable steps?

_____

_____

_____

_____

_____

_____

_____

_____

_____

_____

_____

_____

_____

_____

_____

_____

_____

_____

How can we break Step Three into simpler actionable steps?

_____

_____

_____

_____

_____

_____

_____

_____

_____

_____

_____

_____

_____

_____

_____

_____

_____

_____

How can we break Step Four into simpler actionable steps?

_____

_____

_____

_____

_____

_____

_____

_____

_____

_____

_____

_____

_____

_____

_____

_____

_____

_____

How can we break Step Five into simpler actionable steps?

_____

_____

_____

_____

_____

_____

_____

_____

_____

_____

_____

_____

_____

_____

_____

_____

_____

How can we ensure discipline in these actions?

_____

_____

_____

_____

_____

_____

_____

_____

_____

_____

_____

_____

_____

_____

_____

_____

_____

_____

_____

_____

What are your current wins towards reaching your goal?

_____

_____

_____

_____

_____

_____

_____

How can we ensure more of them?

_____

_____

_____

_____

_____

_____

_____

_____

_____

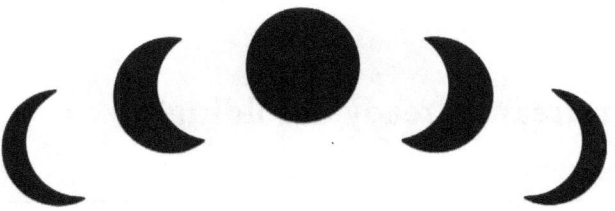

Congratulations Dreamer

"At some point there's no more struggle, just the deep peace that comes from surrendering to a perfection that is beyond your comprehension."

Michael A. Singer

This self-progress journal was designed for YOU to inspire YOU. You have envisioned and embodied your core values and applied them toward your dream of abundant success. I can bet that along the way, there were unexpected twists and turns on your path. But remember, it's all happening FOR you! By radiating gratitude with every step of the way, whether it's today, tomorrow, or sometime in the near future, I guarantee you will look up and see you're already exactly where you want to be.

Thank You for Your Dedication to Achieving Your Dream of Abundant Success

How is your dream already unfolding?

_____

_____

_____

_____

_____

_____

_____

_____

_____

_____

_____

_____

_____

_____

_____

_____

_____

_____

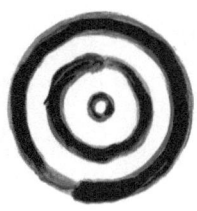

Resources

[1]Young CB, Reddy V, Sonne J. Neuroanatomy, Basal Ganglia. [Updated 2023 Jul 24]. In: StatPearls [Internet]. Treasure Island (FL): StatPearls Publishing; 2025 Jan-. Available from: https://www.ncbi.nlm.nih.gov/books/NBK537141/

[2]Lopes, S., Lima, M., Silva, K. Nature can get it out of your mind: The rumination reducing effects of contact with nature and the mediating role of awe and mood. [Revised 2020 Aug 14]. In: Journal of Environmental Psychology Vol 71 [Internet]: Elsevier; 2020 Aug- Available from: https://doi.org/10.1016/j.jenvp.2020.101489

[3]Arguinchona JH, Tadi P. Neuroanatomy, Reticular Activating System. [Updated 2023 Jul 24]. In: StatPearls [Internet]. Treasure Island (FL): StatPearls Publishing; 2025 Jan-. Available from: https://www.ncbi.nlm.nih.gov/books/NBK549835/

[4]Sender, Ron et al. "Revised Estimates for the Number of Human and Bacteria Cells in the Body." PLoS biology vol. 14,8 e1002533. 19 Aug. 2016, doi:10.1371/journal.pbio.1002533

Funahashi, S. Prefrontal Contribution to Decision-Making under Free-Choice Conditions. [2017 Jul 25]. In: Frontiers Neuroscience Vol 11 [Internet]. Kyoto (Japan): Kokoro Research Center; 2017 Jul-. Available from: https://doi.org/10.3389/fnins.2017.00431

www.ingramcontent.com/pod-product-compliance
Lightning Source LLC
Chambersburg PA
CBHW031256120626
46545CB00007B/2840